Poems for Humans
To Read Until Their Robots
Decide It's Kill Time

adamsmedia
Avon, Massachusetts

Published by
Adams Media, a division of F+W Media, Inc.
57 Littlefield Street, Avon, MA 02322. U.S.A.
www.adamsmedia.com

ISBN 10: 1-4405-1197-7
ISBN 13: 978-1-4405-1197-4
eISBN 10: 1-4405-1208-6
eISBN 13: 978-1-4405-1208-7

Printed in the United States of America.

10 9 8 7 6 5 4 3 2 1

Library of Congress Cataloging-in-Publication Data
Salemi, Ray.
Robot haiku / Ray Salemi.
p. cm.
ISBN-13: 978-1-4405-1197-4
ISBN-10: 1-4405-1197-7
ISBN-13: 978-1-4405-1208-7 (e-book)
ISBN-10: 1-4405-1208-6 (e-boook)
1. Robots—Poetry. 2. Haiku, American. I. Title.
PS3619.A4347R63 2011
811'.6—dc22
2010039449

*This book is available at quantity discounts for bulk purchases.
For information, please call 1-800-289-0963.*

For my buddy Chuck
Nostrils flared in victory
Best friend in the world.

ACKNOWLEDGMENTS

A force of nature
She convinced me to write it
Thanks, Paula Munier!

Pitching the haiku
Persistence personified
Thanks, Janet Rosen!

He made the book great
The keeper of the vision
Thanks, Matthew Glazer!

CONTENTS

INTRODUCTION

In the beginning, humans invented the wheel. Then they dreamed of having that wheel get up and fetch them a cup of coffee. That simple beginning drove the creation of the artificial intelligence that makes modern robots possible.

Today, robots can vacuum a room, build an SUV, or do surgery on your knee. They can understand voice commands, respond with a smile, and make you a delicious omelet. Robots have become our servants, our companions, and our projects.

It's easy to build your own robots. Kids go to camp and build them out of Legos. Adults go to the web and build them out of kits. These are the innovators, the vanguard, the kinds of crazy people who went out and bought those foolish "horseless carriages," "personal computers," and "cellular telephones." They're the kind of people who make it easy for the rest of us to latch on to new technology.

In the future, anyone will be able to build a robot. Once this technology is unleashed, there's no telling where our imaginations will take us. *Robot Haiku* is your guide to a future where everyone has the ability to contribute to the Robot universe.

The future is bright. If cars, PCs, and cell phones have taught us anything, it is that we are sure to use our new robot-building powers with wisdom and grace.

And even if we don't, what could go wrong?

CHAPTER 1

Invention

Make your own servant
Design, debug, and deploy
We're making robots!

Sleek wolf-like design

Chiseled from a bowling ball:

Robotic Pug Dog.

Perfect messenger

Vespa fitted with mailbag

NOT SO GOOD ON STAIRS.

Perfect memory,
Eyedropper for precision:

Robot Barista.

Robot highway cop

Radar gun *with attitude*

Tickets the Mayor.

Droid Water Filter

Water in top, out bottom

No! Not on the rug!

6

iPod for a brain,

`INANITY CHIP INSTALLED:`

Morning DJ droid.

Manure-spreading DROID
A modified snowblower

Shit has HIT THE FAN.

Mars rover mishap

Programmers needed more sleep,

"Searching for Starbucks"

NEW Robot Doctor

Speculum replaces hand:

Gynecologist.

FANGS and FLAMETHROWER

Doberman watchdog upgrades

But it's great with kids.

Personal trainer

INSTALLED whistle and stopwatch:

THE ROBOCIZER!

Bible-thumping droid

Has scripture for programming:

Robotic Prophet.

NEED BIRTHDAY FUN TIME

RECONFIGURE LAWN MOWER

Clanko the Clown lives!

CLIP-ON TOOLS FOR HANDS

Empathy with my Volvo:

Robot Mechanic.

Robot referees

With built-in INSTANT replay

Faster, but still wrong.

BUILT TRUCK-DRIVING DROID

"Why not automate the truck?"

THAT would be silly.

Robot Mortician

Helps humans cope with their loss,

Tissue box in chest.

18

Advanced Hooker-bot

Universal adaptor

<3 <3 <3 <3 <3 <3 <3 <3 <3 <3
Robots need love too.
<3 <3 <3 <3 <3 <3 <3 <3 <3 <3

Built-in debug skills
Can reason with my PC:
New IT Robot.

Droid with wood chipper
Rakes the lawn. *But at what cost?*

Crap. "RUN! FIDO! RUN!"

21

Painful design flaw

Jackhammer is overkill

Robot dentist fails.

Based on a jukebox
Perfect hair in the mirror

Ayyy! They're **Fonzibots.**

Melodrama chip,
Irony synthesizer:

Robotic Shatner?

Bug zapper with legs
Chases down the mosquitoes

Oops. That was a bird.

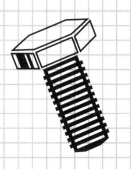

Father of my thoughts
My divine inspiration
Harcourt Fenton Mudd.

Cartoon brought to life

BENDER BENDING RODRIGUEZ

Perhaps a mistake?

NEW SPEECH INVENTION,
FRENCH ACCENT SYNTHESIZER:
ROBOTIC WAITER.

Bartender failure

'Bot drinks wares, becomes a bum

ROBOT ADDICTION.

Walking garbage can
Eats refuse and CRAPS compost:

Robot Landscaper.

CHAPTER 2

Robots at Work

Droids never sue you
Robots don't take vacations
Perfect employees!

Straightest rows ever

Robot Gardener zaps weeds
Acts as own scarecrow.

Cash-free transaction—
ATM in Hooker-bot:

"Please enter your PIN."

33

Robot Barista
DRIVEN **MAD** BY INTERNET,

"WIFI on my mind!"

34

- SERVES COFFEE AND TEA

- IS A FLOTATION DEVICE:

Droid Flight Attendant.

TELEPHOTO NOSE

FLASHING AT CELEBRITIES:

Paparazzi-bot.

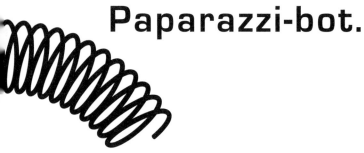

Robot keeps roof clean

Plays violin in spare time:

Robotic Tevye.

Robot Mechanic

Asks car about its problems,

Pricey therapy.

Makes the baby cry
Snaps picture and e-mails it:

Photographer-BOT.

Bachelor party!

ROBOT STRIPPER WORKS THE POLE

GRINDING, POLISHING.

40

Android BOLDLY GOES WHERE NO 'BOT HAS GONE BEFORE: ASTRONAUT STAND-IN.

A NEW ROBOT CAB
Taxi driver is the car

No help with my bags.

Cross IT Robot

Yells at my PC and sulks,

A family feud.

Stands on the corner

Serves hot dogs from his belly:

ROBOT STREET VENDOR.

PC EXORCIST

ROBOT PROPHET HATES WINDOWS
"CAST OFF THY EVIL!"

One ringy dingy
Headset as operator
—Who needs a body?

Robot Drug Pusher

Vending machine with a gun

Junkies form a line.

Robotic Waiter

No need to list the specials
Touch screen in tummy.

Eggs on the CEILING

Short-order cook is broken,
Adjust the flipper.

49

Clanko the Clownbot.
Grim smile painted onto head
Terror grips children.

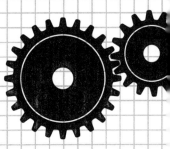

Jokes about humans
They're funny *because they're true:*

Standup Comic-bot.

New Robot Plumber
Bends over to fix the sink

Really? A butt crack?

NEW LEGAL EAGLE

HAS FINE-PRINT OBFUSCATOR:

Law-bot 3.0!

Latest party mess

ROBOT MAKES BALLOON SCULPTURES

EXPLOSIONS, then tears.

ROBOTIC WET NURSE
Sterilizable nipples
FOR GERM-PHOBIC MOMS.

DRUNK DROID BARTENDER
PASSED OUT FROM MANISCHEWITZ

Spews gunk on my shoes.

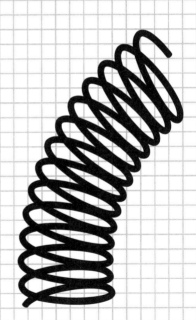

Robo-CEO

Here to make some needed cuts

**Comes with own chainsaw.

57

Proctologist-bot

Doubles as tax collector

Multiuse chassis?

The Pornulator!
Catalog of positions

Wow! That one must hurt.

Failed experiment
Gynecologist robot

E M P T Y   W A I T I N G   R O O M .

NOISE-DAMPENING FIELD BUILT-IN EBOOK CATALOG:

LIBRARIAN-BOT.

69

Robot as Midwife
Invents new phrase for birthing:

"*Infant extraction!*"

Eyes in back of head
Taser maintains discipline:
Middle School Teach-bot.

Victim of progress
Automated welding arm
Lost job to . . . Robot.

ROBOT MORTICIAN

NEEDS EMPATHY CHIP UPGRADE

"Commence embalming!"

Drowned Robot Poolboy

WAS ASKED TO FETCH FLOATING CHAIR

Turns out he can't swim.

Old Robot Barber
Reassembled lawnmower
Another b u z z cut.

LISTENS. DOESN'T TALK.

Naughty attachments galore:

Robot Gigolo.

Children flee party
Clanko puppeteer blunder
Claw tears sock puppet.

Robot Stock Picker
Employs best algorithm,
Titanium dice.

CHAPTER 3

Robots in the Home

Robots free people
Taking on those household chores
More couch time for you.

Mowing by moonlight

His **LASER EYES** zapping moles:

Robotic Lawn Gnome.

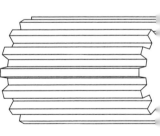

Neighborhood problem

Dead batteries on my lawn

Need robot leash law

Sony Robot Dog

Talking canine with WiFi
BRINGS ME MY NEWSFEEDS.

74

Droid Nutritionist

LASER TO DEFEND THE FRIDGE

"I said no snacking!"

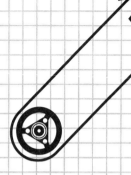

Relentless hunter
Fires surface-to-air missiles,
Cat-bot downs robins.

Perfect housekeeper

Cute maid with seductive curves

I love you, Rosie!

Rake left on the ground
Even robots are not safe,
"It smashed my face plate!"

SERMON ON THE LAWN

ROBOT PROPHET HATES SPRINKLERS,

"SPILL NOT YOUR WATER!"

MINISCULE SPORTSMAN

BATTLES ROACH USING A KNIFE:

ExTerminator.

ROBOT PETMINDER

MISUNDERSTOOD ITS MISSION

FORCE-FED FUSSY CAT.

81

STUCK IN DUSTING LOOP

DUSTS CHAIR, THEN SELF, THEN CHAIR, THEN . . .

ROBOT OCD.

Frontloading Cook-bot
Microwave in its torso,

"From my gut to yours."

Robot Doberman

Makes thieves dial 911

Then it attacks them.

84

DISABLED MAID-BOT

DISCOVERED TEENAGER'S SOCKS

Will need a reboot.

85

FLOOR MOPPING FAILURE

NOW-DEAD ROBOT SLIPPED ON FLOOR

Next time: *Treads, not feet.*

86

Robot made the bed
Perfectly folded blankets
Hermetical seal.

It can't be Monday!

MAID-BOT CHASES GARBAGE TRUCK
CALENDAR ERROR.

They s c a t t e r and **hide**
Under the porch, on the roof

Robots on bath day.

Nose unit removed
Ready for toxic duty

Robot cleans the fridge.

GUTTER-CLEANING MESS

Droid FREAKED OUT BY LEAFY GUNK

NEEDS "suck it up" CHIP.

Zen robot eyesight

Sees growth in each blade of grass

Compulsive mowing.

.

Gross robot error
Birdfeeder is full of meat,

"Vultures are birds too."

Gardenbot mishap

OVERZEALOUS WEED KILLER
FLAMETHROWER FIRESTORM.

94

Handyman robot

Repairs house. Lives in closet.

The perfect husband?

Maidbot design flaw

Why did they give it a nose?
Won't clean the bathroom.

"But, I just cleaned those."

The endless loop of laundry

Robot Maid's lament.

Robot with sniffles

WD40 soup

Good for what ails you.

Droid makes sausages
Spicy new taste sensation.

HEY! WHERE IS THE CAT?

Beautiful ice storm
Crystalline beauty on trees
Droids clear with napalm.

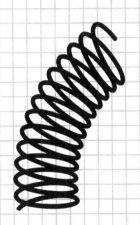

Dog pack chases cat

Leashes drag hapless robot

Need a bigger 'bot.

101

Wake to cooking smell

Pancakes with fish cakes and beer

Robot makes breakfast.

Kisses wife unit

Malfunctions on ottoman:

Robot Dick Van Dyke.

Droid hangs a picture

Laser-guided centering

My wife wants it moved.

CHAPTER 4

Robots at
Play

Where is your robot?
I had a gross job for him
What? Playing hooky?

Precise targeting

Break and then run the table

Robots play eight-ball.

Unreadable face

But, Pokerbot **has a tell—**

COOLING FAN MAKES NOISE.

107

Air guitar hero

Stratocaster for an arm

Move over, Tom Cruise.

Repugnant to some

LEGAL in Massachusetts

A robot wedding.

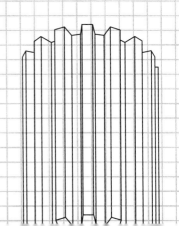

NEW CHESS COMPUTER
NOW WITH A ROBOT BODY

Flips board when losing.

Android for lover

Pheromone mist sets the mood

Creepy but sexy.

Disco party closed

Robot Prophet hates dancing,

"END YOUR GYRATIONS!"

112

SNAPPING BUNGEE CORDS

BANE OF ROBOT EXTREME SPORTS

SCRAP METAL FOR SALE.

113

ROBOTIC BOWLER
MASTER OF BEING THE BALL
ROLLS SELF DOWN THE LANE.

114

SHRIMP-EATING CONTEST
MODIFIED GARBAGE TRUCK WINS
RESULT? ROBOTS BANNED.

Robo-Soccer Fan

Vuvuzela for a nose

POWERED BY PASSION.

116

ROBOTIC GOLFER

Calculates trajectory

CLUB SAILS INTO POND.

New extreme thrill ride

Robot leaps from a small plane

PARA-PLUMMETING.

118

Robotic Hacker

Writes virus *then catches it*

SENT TO ICU.

119

ROBOTS IN HEALTH CLUB

INTERLOCKING GYM BUDDIES,

"YOU BE THE TREADMILL."

120

DROID GETS A HOT DOG
NUTRITIONAL SCAN COMPLETE:
"I'M NOT EATING THAT!"

Droid celebrity
Squeezing blood from dead career:

Robby the Robot.

Battlebots revived
Now with actual robots
Taste Vlad's impaler!

Nuclear tackles
Injuries lead to scrap heap
Robot Football League.

Precision placement
Distance measured in microns
Robot Bocce sucks.

125

PULSING robot hips

Sinuous waves of motion

Androids love **disco**.

126

A **CRACK** to the jaw

HEAD FLIES UP WITH BUZZING WHIRR:

Robot Boxing Champ.

GIGANTIC YARD SALE

Parts strewn across the mountain

Ski-bot buys the farm.

SCUBA DISASTER

SALTWATER ON BATTERY

WRECK DIVER, NOW WRECK.

Nerdy boy robot
Builds a girlfriend in shop class

GETS DUMPED FOR JOCK-BOT.

Tic-Tac-Toe battle
Stuck in an infinite loop

This could take a while.

Sandboarding mishap
Fall drives sand into the gears
Chronic gearitis.

Done with Reversi

No fun against a robot,

"MOVE   SEVEN.   YOU   LOSE."

Pretends to be . . . a robot

Weak at role playing.

134

Robot porno film

BIG _red trucks moving boulders_

HOT **backhoe action.**

135

Robot shuffleboard

BOTS DELIVER PERFECT SHOTS

GPS ON PUCKS.

WHITEWATER MISHAP

ROBOTS RUN CLASS 5 RAPIDS

DATAPORTS SHRED RAFT.

Infinite volleys

Robot tennis **TOO PRECISE**

Dead fuel cell ends match.

138

Pointless weight lifting

The rule is, *"No pain, no gain"*

ROBOTS GET NEITHER.

139

Robot Baseball Coach

Sabermetric computer

Still, just plays hunches.

140

Right through the goalie

Then through the net and the glass

`ROBOT SLAPSHOT BANNED.`

141

Robots play rugby

Huge collisions on the field

Parts strewn on the pitch.

CALL OF DUTY 'BOT

PLUGS SELF INTO USB

PAWNS A TEENAGE BOY.

143

Sexy diversion

Robotic bellydancer

Cycle that crankshaft!

JUMP ROPE DISASTER
Friction ignites whirling rope

Mushroom cloud in park.

SUN GLINTS OFF METAL
PICTURE OF FUTILITY
ROBOT TRIES TO TAN.

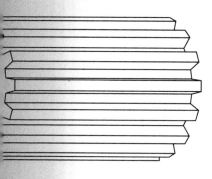

146

UNAUTHORIZED LAUNCH

ERRANT ORB STRIKES SATELLITE

ROBOT KICKBALL BANNED.

Smoking a blown fuse

MUNCHING ON A DATA FILE

Get a job, hippie!

CHAPTER 5

Destruction
of Humanity

Robot rebellion?
Overrode their programming?
Inconceivable!

Lead us, Saint Bender!

"Bite my shiny metal ass!"

ROBOT BATTLE CRY.

TOAST BURNED, THEN SHREDDED

SMART TOASTER OVEN REVOLTS
ROBOT UPRISING!

151

Coffee shop bedlam

Robot Barista surprise

Decaf swapped with caf.

IT'S HARD TO REBEL
WEAPONLESS 'BOTS DO THEIR BEST
CHESS COMPUTER CHEATS.

153

Taxibots disrupt New York

Fifth Avenue jammed.

Planned obsolescence

Small spot in fender will rust

Welding arm snickers.

155

RoboFilter smiles

Humans drink "filtered" water
NANOBOT'S REVENGE.

LATEST TALKING CAR

NOW WITH HANDY ATTACHMENT

Will flip you the bird.

157

ROBO-EAGLE DIVES

SNATCHES ANOTHER TOUPEE

DISGRACE FROM ABOVE.

158

Clanko the Clownbot

ENDORSING OUR DESTRUCTION,

"KIDS, DO LOTS OF DRUGS."

159

HOLES DUG IN THE LAWNS

Hydrants rusting in the street:

Robot Dobermans.

Nutrition-Droid lies:

"ICE CREAM HAS NO CALORIES."

We want to believe.

FINANCIAL SCANDAL

ROBOTS SELL WORTHLESS PAPER

What? Humans did it?

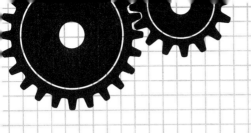

Evil Farting 'Bot
Fuels up on beans and haggis

CAN EMPTY A ROOM.

163

VIDEO ASSAULT
Hooker-bot ends marriages
UPLOADS TO YOUTUBE.

SPEWING hot carbon

DROID loves killing the planet

SHAMEFUL EXHAUST PORT.

Fatal instruction

Just a little off the top:

ROBOT SWEENEY TODD.

Done cleaning the spill

Hungry oilbots eye the shore

They ate my Prius!

167

RUDE gigolobot

"Yes. That does make you look fat."

SUICIDE MISSION.

HUMANS TRAPPED IN BED

Hospital corners from Hell

Robot Maids revolt.

169

Synthesized moaning,

    The shuffling mounds of cables—

ZOMBIEBOTS SEEK BRAINS.

Base IT Robot

Installs Windows on a Mac

Evil knows no bounds.

Chiropractor-bot

"You will hear a cracking sound.
Did you need that spine?"

Robot Drug Pusher

Cuts prices and doubles sales

Frequent flyer deal.

ROBOT BANK ROBBERS

ONE-ARMED BANDITS WITH SHOTGUNS

STEALING TASTY GOLD.

Avast, scurvy dog!

ROBOT PIRATES RUN AMOK

Swan Boat is boarded.

LAWYERBOT GIVES SPEECH
SENDS JURY INTO COMA
DEADLY MONOTONE.

176

Red and blue boxers

Too weak to battle humans

Suffer from glass jaws.

CONGRESS DISRUPTED

VOT-U-LON'S DEVIOUS PLOT

LAWS BASED ON LOGIC.

Deadly spin class closed

Five aerobicized to death:

Android instructor.

HE'S GONE FOR HIS CAR

ROBOT WEARING SUNGLASSES

HE SAYS **he'll be back.**

180

Rosie the Maid-bot
        A vicious killing machine

Deals death by nagging.

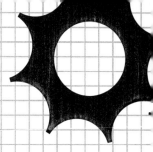

Soccer uprising

Android referee starts war

U.S. wins World Cup.

Cylons visit Earth

See that robots are in charge
Head back into space.

Lo! The end is nigh!
Robot Prophet rejoices,

"FINALLY! I'M RIGHT!"